FAMILIES

My Brother and Sister

Katie Dicker

WAYLAND

Explore the world with **Popcorn** - your complete first non-fiction library.

Look out for more titles in the Popcorn range. All books have the same format of simple text and striking images. Text is carefully matched to the pictures to help readers to identify and understand key vocabulary. www.waylandbooks.co.uk/popcorn

Published in paperback in 2014 by Wayland
Copyright © Wayland 2014

Wayland
Hachette Children's Books
338 Euston Road
London NW1 3BH

Wayland Australia
Level 17/207 Kent Street
Sydney NSW 2000

 Produced for Wayland by
White-Thomson Publishing Ltd
www.wtpub.co.uk
+44 (0)843 208 7460

All rights reserved.
Editor: Katie Dicker
Designer: Amy Sparks
Picture researchers: Katie Dicker
Series consultant: Kate Ruttle
Design concept: Paul Cherrill

British Library Cataloging in Publication Data
Dicker, Katie.
   My brother and sister. -- (Popcorn)
   1. Brothers and sisters--Juvenile literature.
   I. Title II. Series
   306.8'75-dc22

ISBN: 978 0 7502 8869 9

Wayland is a division of Hachette Children's Books,
an Hachette UK company.
www.hachette.co.uk

Printed and bound in China

10 9 8 7 6 5 4 3 2 1

Picture Credits: **Corbis**: Eric Audras/PhotoAlto 17, Image Source 19; **Dreamstime**: Monkey Business Images cover/1/4/11/21, Photomyeye 5/22r, Elena Elisseeva 6/22l, Marzanna Syncerz 8, Tatyana Gladskikh 18; **Getty Images**: Michael DeLeon 9, Floresco Productions 13, William Hart 14, Jack Hollingsworth 16; **iStockphoto**: Judy Lynn 2/15, Maica 10/22m, Caracter 12; **Photolibrary**: Norbert Schaefer 20; **Shutterstock**: Monkey Business Images 7.

Every effort has been made to clear copyright.
Should there be any inadvertent omission,
please apply to the publisher for rectification.

Contents

What is a brother or sister?

A brother or sister is someone who has the same parent as you. Brothers and sisters are sometimes called siblings.

Sophie has one sister and one brother.

Some people have no brothers or sisters. They are known as an only child.

How many brothers or sisters do you have?

Tanya is an only child, but she has lots of friends to play with.

Half brothers and sisters

Joe lives with his birth mum and dad. He has a half sister called Sally. Sally has a different birth dad. Joe is Sally's half brother.

Joe and Sally have the same birth mum, but their birth dads are different.

Sally goes to visit her birth dad at the weekend. He lives with his new partner, Anna. They've just had a baby daughter called Jessica.

Jessica is Sally's new half sister.

Step brothers and sisters

Some people have step siblings. When Jenny's birth dad married Kate, she became Jenny's stepmum. Kate's two children became Jenny's step brother and step sister.

Jenny became a step sister to Sam and Freya when Jenny's dad married their mum, Kate.

Jenny

Dad

Kate

Sam

Freya

Ben's mum died when he was young. Now Ben has a stepmum and a new step brother, called Frank.

A step brother or a step sister can be like a new friend to play with.

Step brothers and step sisters can be the same age!

Twins

Jack and Tom are twins. They were born within an hour of each other, to the same birth mum and dad.

Some twins are identical. This means they look exactly the same.

Jack and Tom share the same birthday.

Yasmine and Otis are twins, but they don't look exactly like each other. They are non-identical twins.

Do you know any twins? Do they look similar?

Different ages

Older brothers and sisters often take care of their younger siblings. They can teach them some of the things they know.

Maya's big sister, Lily, is showing Maya how to cook.

Why do you think some people like being the oldest child?

Some younger brothers or sisters get a lot of attention. This may be because they need more help doing things.

Would you like to be the youngest, oldest or middle child?

Respect and kindness

Sometimes, it can be hard to get on with a brother or sister. You may not like them sharing your bedroom or playing with your toys.

Jake was happy when his sister said he could have the top bed.

If you want your siblings to be kind to you, you have to treat them in a nice way too. This is called showing respect.

Lottie often shares her book with her brother, Adam.

Learning to get along

Although you love your brother or sister, you may feel cross about something they have done. Sometimes, you may fight or argue.

It is okay to argue, as long as you say sorry and make up afterwards.

Arguing with a sibling doesn't mean you don't love them.

In order to get along, family members need to talk and listen to each other to find out how everyone is feeling.

Talking about the things that upset you can usually help to solve the problem.

Jealous feelings

It is normal to sometimes feel jealous of your brother or sister. You may think that your parents are not treating you fairly.

Oliver thought that his sister was getting all his parents' attention.

Talk to your parents about how you are feeling. Together you can work out ways to help you feel better again.

Becky's dad makes time for her, while her mum and sister are playing.

Everyone is special

Although you cannot choose
your brothers and sisters, they
can be your friends as you
grow up and get older.

Bill has been friends with his brother Ted for over 70 years!

Your siblings are part of
your family. You care for
them and they care for you.
This makes them very special.

How do you like to spend time with your siblings?

Sibling study

1. Look at these photographs showing some of the children featured in this book. Can you answer these questions? Look back through the book if you need a reminder.

1. How is Joe related to Sally?

2. Does Tanya have any sisters?

3. What is special about Jack and Tom's birthday?

22

Answers: 1. Joe is Sally's half brother. He has the same birth mum as Sally, but his birth dad is different.
2. Tanya doesn't have any sisters. She is an only child.
3. Jack and Tom's birthday is on the same day because they are twins.

2. If you have a brother or sister, take a photograph or draw a picture of them.

Write down five things you like about living with them. If you don't have a sibling, draw and write about one of your friend's brother or sister.

Stick your descriptions around the drawings or photographs to show what it's like to live with a brother or sister.

Someone to play with

Can help each other

Can ask to borrow their things

Show them your list. Can the siblings do the same for you?

Glossary

argue to fall out with someone

birth dad the man who made you with your birth mum

birth mum the woman who made you with your birth dad

birth parents your birth mum and birth dad

half brother/sister a brother or sister who shares one birth parent with you

married when two people become husband and wife

partner the person that an adult loves and chooses to live with

respect to show that you care for someone by treating them in a nice way

sibling a brother or a sister

step brother/sister a brother or sister who doesn't have the same birth parents as you

stepmum a woman who is not your birth mum, but who marries your birth dad

twins brothers or sisters born on the same day in the same year

Index